66 galaxie

The Katherine Bakeless Nason Literary Publication Prizes

The Bakeless Literary Publication Prizes
are sponsored by the Bread Loaf Writers'
Conference of Middlebury College to support
the publication of first books. The manuscripts
are selected through open competition and
are published by University Press of New
England/Middlebury College Press.

➤ *Competition Winners in Poetry*

1996
Mary Jo Bang, *Apology for Want*
judge: Edward Hirsch

1997
m loncar, *66 galaxie*
judge: Garret Hongo

66 galaxie

poems by

m loncar

➤ *A Middlebury / Bread Loaf Book*

Published by University Press of New England

Hanover and London

Middlebury College Press
Published by University Press of New England, Hanover, NH 03755
Printed in the United States of America
5 4 3 2 1
CIP data appear at the end of the book

"hey locked-boy" appears in *caliban* #15

"timothy and angelina crash" appears in *soundings east* #20

"giving my head to the mississippi," "insomnia," and "wallace p hipslit, age nine, foot loose and fancy free, standing on a swing; about to break his leg" appear in *spinning jenny* #1

"our father (the world's foremost authority on jelly roll morton)" appears in *spinning jenny* #2

"picasso shag" appears in *a visit to the gallery*

a c k n o w l e d g m e n t s

much thanks (indebtedness) to my family and a number of people who
helped me with the galaxie including r tillinghast t moss s alcosser
s messer k tuma c e harrison h barrows c barnet r sedliar
(for the underwood) and especially r mcdaniel

thanks to the reids (especially cooper)
josh, millie, and alan in youngstown
e carlson in providence j kessler and m peters in ny
m murray, d mcarthur, and j herman in san fran
the mannings in georgia

thanks to the cover artwork contributors
calligrapher   yong xu
photographer   d coombe
model   k breslin

everyone at university press of new england

"a good disaster" was written for k mah
"hollywood" for the photographer m powell
"giving my head" for c brandel "b street" for n roemer
"tim and ang" for t loncar & c barnet
"hey locked boy" for n petersen and n heidrich
"the sky-high motel" for m bada & stu
"picasso shag" for marko

you should send (craziness) poems to c e harrison
at spinning jenny po box 1492 cooper station ny, ny 10276

poems

➤ for h barrows and j reiss

66 galaxie

one night america: a boy and his blowtorch

will tear through you with his tangled
fingernails and sour memories   open   filled
4 bleeding hearts in his chest   you'll throw
daughters and sons and black coffee at him
but he'll stare at each and weep and worship
their bodies are like machines to him   and he'll
be trying to love them without erections like
he wanted just to inhale them for a minute
and they'll love him all the more   because
in america   they love crucifixions   flat
squirrels and birds   those things and of course
evangelists and mass murderers and movie stars
i myself like those people plenty you know
but no one as much as tina turner who has been
known to at times take control of this steering wheel
and might i add i have been known to have enjoyed
the rides   and as for that blowtorch   he always
liked to leave the people he loved   something to
remember him by   sometimes a wired metal headboard
above their bed   or sometimes   even something small
like iron railroad tracks running through their kitchens

for wings
or for an end

rilke

Giving My Head To The Mississippi

It's just you
and me and
the hatchet
baby.

We've come to hear Coltrane
as she lifts off my shirt, Leadbelly
when she smiles, smoothes
mud across my chest

and sips

a brainpanfull of
a drowning man's
memories says
splendid;
nightmarish.

This
is the twenty-third day of my life in America
without you baby

and i've eased into new
addictions, like saying "baby"
all the time and whistling
at Angelina through
my teeth as a man in
a big blue Plymouth drives

off the Martin Luther King Jr bridge.

4

hey locked boy

she
    slipped in
the clear soak of her
    hair just washed-up
into the car   and
    against your mouth

        boy
       do you like bourbon?

    moved
her fingers toward
    the wheel   rolled
 down the windows
and started the car
    you're ill   and now
she's driving playing
    with her hair
       whispering

       this fucking moon is
       pulling
          me apart too

ohio

besides spilling the better half, as well as the steamier half,
  of mcdonald's best try at a cup of coffee on my crotch,
   the ride out of ohio passed without incident.

Toad Highway

go ahead
place the girl on
your lap   you

can operate the pedals   she'll turn

the steering wheel   you'll
come within inches of
hitting a boy named
Marshall

who's deaf in the middle of the road

with a toy
machine gun
blam blam blam
you're dead
he adds as

Angelina turns around to see
a big blue Plymouth speeding
off the ramp from toad highway

tell me about him

my father?

baby
he hung
the fucking moon.

Cops and Robbers

Pig shit   she says   *pig shit*
passing harshman's hog farm
driving on 9 but it's 2 am
and it's the all oldies show
        and there's
less talk just the music
dead people love

            i'd look good in a
                tazmanian mink

                        yep   you would

smiling she imagines
you all decked out dancing
drinking the place dry
insulting the duchess
punching out the count
tipping your hat   hooked
into her arms

            my skin really shines
                under pearls

                        like polished chrome
                        i'd bet

she stops the car   takes
a deep breath   *pig shit*
ambles over and unlocks the trunk
you get out and walk over to the passenger
seat   she starts the car and drives off
you rest your head on her shoulder
   and whisper

      when we get to omaha
        let's play cops and robbers

the sky-high motel at midnight

when the boy
    stretched-out on the bed
gets an erection   someone
    smacks it with a hammer
            there
    how do you like that?

it might be the girl with
    a texas drawl   that says
            "i can't hear the tv!!"
    or the boy from kentucky
who walks with a cane
    and wears old gangster suits
            from the forties

they'll drink coffee
    and watch ida lupino movies
            all night   and whisper

        yes   yes   that's good!
        pass me the pornography
            atta girl!   and

    i think soon it's going to rain

peoria

we were drinking coffee (of course)   when in walks
these two punk rockers   one full of body piercings
and nails in his skin   the other with a blood orange red
mohawk   smoking a pipe   the one with the nails also has
a dog collar around his neck and hands the leash to angelina
who flattered   starts leading him all around the place   circling
tables   and into the bathroom   then the one smoking the pipe
(it musta been about 200 degrees)   comes up to me and says
listen here kid

    we're worried about you
    we love you and we
    don't want anything to happen to you
    everything will be all right
    it'll be ok

kisses me

then gets up   grabs the leash from angelina
leads the one with the nails in him
and they get in their van and drive off

jesus tim   sometimes i have no idea
            what the hell is going on

kentucky

hello sir   i'm glad you're here we
were just trying to pet the cows and
have a little fun with the electric fence boy
we didn't mean to trouble anyone least of all
the owner of such a fine looking field and my but
that is a fine looking cow you have there as well as
a fine looking pasture   in this light it almost looks quite
blue   they really do have blue grass here don't they that's what
i hear blue grass and not a whole set of teeth in the state

charlie shivers

walked into a road
house   started shaking

his problem was
in the middle of illinois

he realized
how alone he was

started missing
his brother and his brother's gal

yeah
he was all alone out there

madame

what is it about fucking you that reminds me
    of reading with my bifocals upside down?

lip-balm telephone tornado motorcycle

your body rhymes
   with her body like mine
rhymes with lighter fluid
   lip-balm   telephone
     tornado motorcycle
          prosthetic-limb

sickos

you know these five guys in an apartment watching an evil porn f
ilm when another guy walks in   and is repulsed and belts out
"where did you get that bullshit?" and one of the boys watching
says "i stole it from the neighbor's mailbox" and he says "man
you sure got some sick neighbors!"

God always gives the best gifts   just when you need it
a jukebox in davenport
full of patsy cline

Timothy and Angelina Crash

I.
more than
about anything   i'd like
to tell you

that
my brother drove
a 66 galaxie

or
a 64 dart with
fins

that'd
separate hydrogen from
oxygen

truth is
he drove a 78
oldsmobile

he got it
from our grandfather on his
16th birthday

II.

tim's like jesus
three days too late
holding his hands
against her chest
placing his mouth
on the lips of
a cold dead fish

III.

oh yeah they was crazy sons a bitches drivin all around like they
owned

        the road   like it was theirs   like god gave it to 'em

IV.

there's a train from nanjing
headed towards harbin and you're
throwing up next to a very old woman
named li lao shi   she's holding your
hair away from your face   is trying
to get you to drink some water and
you're thinking it might not be so bad
to die on a train

V.

i remember one time at this family picnic my uncle
chet asked us what we wanted to be when we grew
up   i said a fireman   tim said   *anything but bored baby*

how can you compete with that?

VI.

tim brought her home once
yeah   i told him   she has that
70's soft porn meets 20's flapper
with a bit of josephine baker in paris
thrown in   not too bad
if you like that sort of thing

the truth is
she was garbo
all the way

VII.

it was in northern california   pacifica
  a stray ford   leslie campolito said   that ran
        out into the street in front of them and they
            swerved off the road into

the ravine   flipped four or five times before hitting
        a family of deer   roger clatterbuck swears it
            was outside mexico city   a ford as well but that the boy
                thrown into the street lamp   buttered up against

the girl afterwards   they were ok   he swears without
        4 or 5 bruises between them   it was those mexican
        hospitals   that released her   they ate a fine dinner
                and a late night too but when the boy woke up
                        in the morning she was dead

VIII.

        the hotel maid is climbing
        the stairs to clean the room
        registered to the crashes

                angelina and timothy

IX.

in the middle of manchuguo you wrote me
a letter about the mongolian children that
stopped your train   that it was cold and that
you were sick   they were naked with skin
leathered by the wind and smiling and playing
some crazy game dodging trains   and that you
couldn't really stand to think about marlon
brando right now   or tina turner   but that
sometimes   you'd think about buster keaton
holding that umbrella in steamboat bill jr

X.
more than
about anything   i'd like
to tell you

that
my brother drove
a 66 galaxie

there goes the bride

a woman fresh off the train
and already i get orders   *so you're*
the new caretaker?

after all   it's an easy country
to lose your way in

what
with all those snakecharmers
(in the bicarbonate belt)
wailing

like a sinner on revival day
(aww
it's not the sex
that's killing me

it's
the sentimentalism)

nothing that is helpful
hardly anything useful

rilke

Wallace P. Hipslit, age nine, foot loose and fancy free, standing on a swing; about to break his leg

The chance to impress
a girl like Aemijlia Neckpotter
comes once in a lifetime

why
       not
              leap

why
       not
              bend

begins
the hypnotist
swingset   laughing
its head off

men agree
men are mean
men agree
men are green
screams the grass

the scratch and sniff scents of an early June;
whispering

     why   why   why   why
         stop   stop   stop   stop

             Wallace

as my cat eats the head of a field mouse he has caught

i can only think of him as
a kitten on my head, that strange
way my brother and i used to carry him
walking around the living room the way
egyptian women bring water into villages. is this
the root incident of his head problem/fetish? is this
the event that led him to hate heads? i remember when i
ate my first head. it was certainly not out of hatred,
more a curiosity, like what's under her
skirt, what's going on in her head as she
lifts it and I catch the echo of my body
hitting the floor.

insomnia

it starts
   inevitably
as something
    small:
the suicide of a friend
your team's loss in
   the World Series   a
     chipped tooth

first the cackle
of the echolaliac
in the bath and

then

above the din of
her heaving chest
when you're about to
close your eyes

you hear it:

a nest of thin
itchy trigger fingers
rustling at the end
of your arm

for me

it starts as
something

small

still life without moosehead

confused?
(flabbergasted!)
everyone's upset because
the goddamned moosehead

didn't even get in
the photograph

fly
papered against her tv
she'll be up all night
waiting for someone to
tell her why

it makes a difference.

our father (the world's foremost
authority on jelly roll morton)

the (good) doktor   confirmed
              our suspicians

        melancholia typicalia

   a permanent condition
                (and traditional!)

        "look at any of 'em
           kicking in the cage"
                (aww
        just
      toss 'em a bottle doc
        and you watch 'em

              warm right up)

a fake kiss (a bullettrap)
the grill of a detroit car

gravity (all

nonsense now)

cut-up

and opened at the repair shop

come spy with me

(i

socked him in the jaw

and beat it) he died

on his knees

barking like a mad dog

(forgive me

and poor so and so)

the game upstairs

is not to fall

in love

(a shiny toy

on the outside)

wildcatters and sobs

as far as i'm concerned
         there are 2 types of
      saps   in the world   and then

   a (true) straight 6 jacket (calm)

      as she gives me
   the ol   i'm in the same boat nod

**there's nothing
  (like a good disaster!)
    for sorting things out**

my trials have not yet ended
                let's
          make it a seduction scene
                    (aww

    this street's all the time
            yellin

        get yourself a girl
          and hold her tight)
            where?

        you been all my life
            aggie?

tim i

have been thinking
     about our question
can a man have sex
     without an erection
and would have to say
     from my experience

     not really

lonely america

she mentioned 'worthless'
& he took it in

berryman

if they hang you(good
morning angel)

god spoke god (said nothing)

  and waited
    a long time too . . .

  "i've got ideas
you doing ballet

    me doing comedy"

flashback to hotel sex scene (or
   how my trousers ended up in new jersey)

somebody bit off somebody's
   nipple
   and then

i couldn't remember anything
      except

are you sure i'm not going to hurt anybody?

            starts car   then leaves

43

otto dago
(with a cuban accent)

just walked off

might be

in a diner somewhere

(might be

in a funeral parlour)

the tank top t-shirt, the saxophone
  the ceaseless blaze of the neon flashing

& whatever moonlight
        happens
    to seep through
        the window

the hollywood knickerbocker hotel suicide

lonely america

dressing and undressing

again

lonely?

the slow strip tease?

be good(and kisses

and caresses)

postscript: landscape with car crash

```
toadhighwaytoadhighwaytoadhighwaytoadhighway
toadhighwaytoadhighwaytoadhighwaytoadhighwaytoadhighwaytoadhighway
ra                                    toadhighwaytoadhighwaytoad
 mp
 ramp ra
 mp ramp                                    cefencefencefencefe
l          l                    encefen              nc
e          e                    f              efenc
f          fdrivewaydrivewaydrivewaydrivewaydrive      car
f          f                    f    driveway      tractor  cat
i          i                    e    ho
n          n                    n    use
g          g                    c              cow
w          w                    f              cowcow
e          e                    e                        co
l          l                    n
l          l                    ce
r car      r                    f              ba    cow
o ca       o                    e              rn
a r marshaall police car        n
d ambulancde police car         c                        cow
lpolice car  l                  e                        cow cow
e          e                    f
f          f                    e
f          f                    n
i          i                    c
n          n                    e
g          g                    f
w          w                    e
e          e                    n
l          l    mr brandel      c
l          l    angelina        e
r          r                    f
o          o                    e
 a          a                   n
  d          d
```

what shall i do with my mouth?

rilke

repeating the word girl

writing a poem about the girl should never be better
　　　than the girl　　　than being with the girl

don't write the poem about the girl
　　　unless you'd really rather be with the girl

picasso shag

      sad?
     (admit it)
   you liked her (blue) kitchen
smoking all night and drinking coffee
     (she'd place a raisin in each cup)

     admit it
   you liked her (sad)
way of ransacking the place
    best (how 'bout a cigarette
        babe?)

the king of refrigerator poems

eye
the king of refrigerator
poems

former
socialist vegetarian teenage
republican

3 time
consecutive winner of the goya award for
moroseness

       poetic hardass
       blessed with a blatant disregard for form punctuation
       capitalization as well as a willingness to fuck with any
       margin foolish enough to come within yards
       of me

closet manic
depressive political passive aggressive romantic poolshark
(cheats at card games)

midnight to
3am prank phone call
aficionado

master
dj mixtape
master

chronic
put out his cigar in your gin thank
you
                              (let's not forget poetic hardass)

former
conspirator confidant lover and co-
pilot

narcissistic 90's beatnik
pit barbecue peroghi lover and kentucky
blintzes   smooth

scatterbrained
super-genius
(don't make me
show you my
g r e scores)
control freak
commercial
welding
fetish-boy
(let's not stop me when i'm on a roll)

don't
hassle me with your line break suggestions
bucko

fascist neo-
formalist   nightmare
candidate

convicted
of high crimes against the queen edmund
spenser is not edmund wilson edmund spenser
is not edmund wilson edmund spenser is not edmund
wilson (sure
he is)

bridge-boy
hip hellcat hard to figure bizarre just figure plain old fashioned
annoying

scary scared scarred (don't believe him)

i can help you

now

if you called right now and told me
you fucked it up you love me the whole
thing needs to change you are so sorry
for everything could still be worked out

i would tell you that i just got done
wringing my eyes up late feeling so sad
that the world seemed smaller than me and

my collection of aging metaphors again
laid out so low and insignificant and there is

a patsy cline song about me
my heart   a poem
about pissing blood an hour after
my car ceased to be one of the living

psychos out there with a sense of humor
why don't you call now   and tell me how
you were so fucked up feeling sad that
when he took you in his arms it was
easier because he was there and he had
arms but in the end was

handless   i won't even think about
the year without erections and the green-haired
girl who tried all sorts of crazy things that
we could laugh about after i got done believing in god and

thanking him and worshipping the son of a bitch for
the big ditch of the midwest that keeps on going till you
look at it and realize you'd be better off without the sweet
swell of her forearm up against your back   better off without

your head and writing all those poems that rhyme
and have a french word like "   " in it just to make the people
who haven't been there feel worse

about leaving the scars numbered for the reader's
convenience like #54B56 (right forehead) or everyone's
favorite #23C71(left front cheek) so if someone has talked

some sense it sure as hell hasn't been me fucking
up my life   waiting for you   because everyone especially

rich is so goddamn sick of seeing you behind every fucking
line and always wearing that same stupid outfit and pushing
those same buttons that eradicate little bits of my soul everytime
i so much as think about enjoying a song or getting some sleep
or writing a poem about my father or the landscape of
new hampshire on one of those still quiet nights

that seem to inspire all those poets who've never even heard of
all the post modern tv scrap culture generation x bullshit
that i have to wear hipboots to wade through

       i'm dreaming i can understand you

endowed with

  an absolute clarity

      i had better stop now

  i can help you baby

b street souflaki

if we were together for your birthday i'd take you out to eat at some
greek place called little athens or b street souflaki or something and
we'd order salads with bitter olives and feta with warm bread and
we'd have some wine and then i'd take out a cigarette and try and
look dashing and then maybe zeus would stretch out his arm above me
so you could see that   hey   it was ok with the gods of olympus
if you wanted to be with me

OR:
tempting fate
on a basic level

notes

"for wings or for an end"
     from "Girl's Lament"
          Rainer Maria Rilke

"almost nothing that is helpful, hardly anything useful."
     from *Letters to a Young Poet*
          Rainer Maria Rilke

"she mentioned 'worthless' & he took it in"
     from *Dream Song* #109
          John Berryman

"what shall i do with my mouth?"
     from "The Poet"
          Rainer Maria Rilke

University Press of New England publishes books under its own imprint and is the publisher for Brandeis University Press, Dartmouth College, Middlebury College Press, University of New Hampshire, Tufts University, and Wesleyan University Press.

Library of Congress Cataloging-in-Publication Data

Loncar, M., 1968–
  66 galaxie / M. Loncar.
    p. cm.
  "The Katharine Bakeless Nason Literary Publication Prizes"—
  T.p. verso.
  ISBN 0–87451–877–6 (cloth : alk. paper).—
  ISBN 0–87451–878–4 (pbk : alk. paper)
  I. Title
PS3562.O484A6I4   1998
811'.54—dc21   98–17474